My First
Horse and Pony Book

KINGFISHER

a Houghton Mifflin Company imprint
222 Berkeley Street
Boston, Massachusetts 02116
www.houghtonmifflinbooks.com

First published in 2005
10 9 8 7 6 5 4 3

3TR/0706/LFG/CLSN(CLSN)/140MA/F

ISBN 0-7534-5878-0
ISBN 978-07534-5878-5

Printed in China

Author: Judith Draper
U.K. consultant: Elwyn Hartley Edwards
U.S. consultant: Lesley Ward
Editors: Russell Mclean, Stephanie Pliakas, Jennifer Schofield
Designer: Poppy Jenkins
Photographer: Matthew Roberts
Hair and makeup: Isobel Bulat
Picture research manager: Cee Weston-Baker
Production manager: Nancy Roberts
DTP manager: Nicky Studdart
DTP operator: Sarah Pfitzner
Proofreader and indexer: Sheila Clewley

Clothing and equipment supplied by
Dublin, Cuddly Ponies, and Roma.

Ponies supplied and produced by
Justine Armstrong-Small BHSAI,
pictured with Zin Zan (Champion
Working Hunter and Supreme Horse,
Horse of the Year Show 2003;
Reserve Champion, Royal
International; Champion
Working Hunter, Horse
of the Year Show 2004).

My First
Horse and Pony Book

Judith Draper

KINGFISHER

BOSTON

Contents

What are horses and ponies?

Horses and ponies are both members of the horse family, which also includes donkeys and zebras. A pony is smaller than a horse and has shorter legs. Horses and ponies are many different sizes and colors, depending on which breed they belong to.

Horse

Pony

Measuring up

To find out how tall your horse or pony is, measure it at the withers. These are the top of the animal's shoulders, between its neck and back. You can measure it in hands or in inches.

On the withers

This sliding bar lets you see the horse or pony's height. Rest it on the highest point of the withers.

Made to measure

This special pole is called a measuring stick. _____

No shoes

To find your horse or pony's true height, stand it on level ground. It should not be wearing shoes.

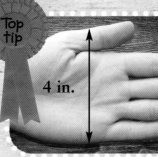

Top tip

4 in.

Hands

One hand equals around four inches (10cm), which is around the width of an adult's hand.

Points of a horse and pony

Each part of a horse or pony's body has its own special name. These are known as the "points" of the animal. You will recognize some of the names, such as knee and elbow, because they describe parts of our bodies too.

Kind eyes
When you choose a horse or pony, look for one with big eyes and a kind expression. This usually means that it is friendly.

croup

dock

back

hindquarters

tail

flank

hind leg

belly

Hock
This joint works like your ankle. Horses and ponies need strong hocks in order to carry the weight of a rider and to jump.

heel

Hoof and sole
A horse's foot has a hard covering called the hoof. The part underneath the foot is called the sole.

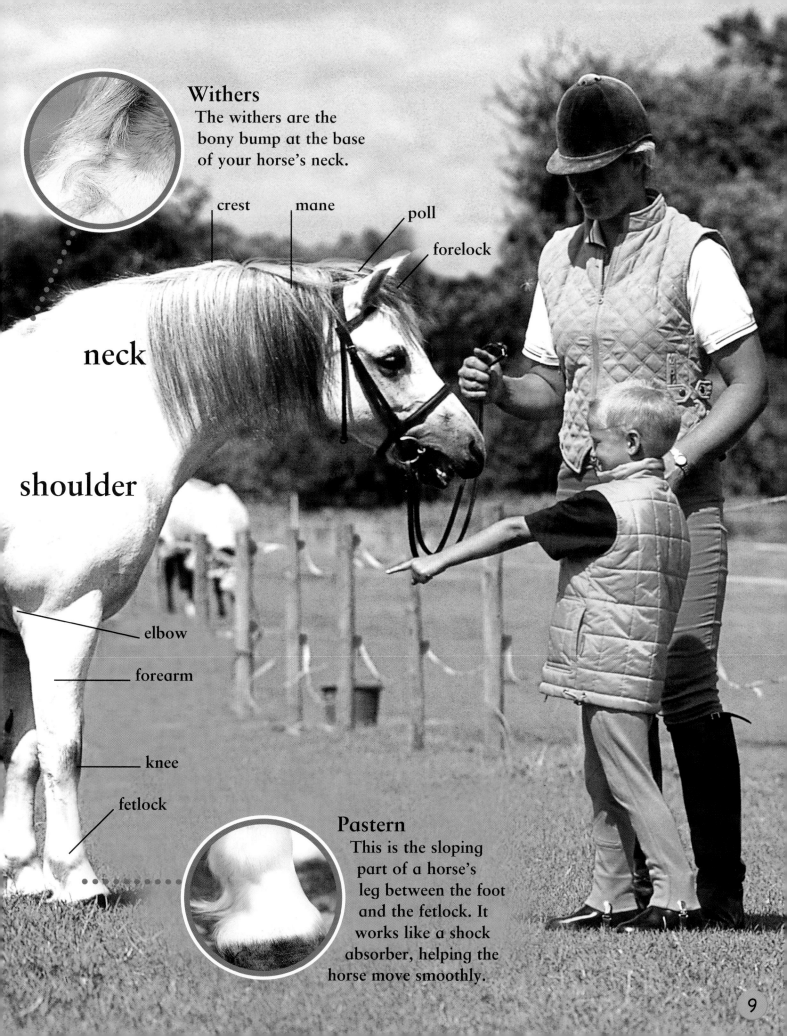

Withers
The withers are the bony bump at the base of your horse's neck.

crest

mane

poll

forelock

neck

shoulder

elbow

forearm

knee

fetlock

Pastern
This is the sloping part of a horse's leg between the foot and the fetlock. It works like a shock absorber, helping the horse move smoothly.

Horse and pony breeds

There are more than 150 different breeds and types of horses and ponies. A "breed" is a horse or pony group that has been bred carefully over a period of time. A "type" is a horse or pony that is used for a specific purpose such as a hunter or an equitation pony.

Stock Horse
The tough and fast Australian Stock Horse is used for cattle herding. Until 200 years ago there were no horses in Australia, so the Stock Horse is a mixture of breeds from other countries.

Arabian
The Arabian is the oldest and purest of all horse breeds. It is small and strong and moves with a beautiful "floating" action. Arabians are high-spirited and playful but are gentle, too.

Haflinger
This sturdy pony is named after a mountain village in Austria. It is sure-footed and makes a good riding or driving pony. All Haflingers are chestnut in color.

Thoroughbred

This is the fastest breed of horse in the world and makes a perfect racehorse. Thoroughbreds are strong, but they can be nervous and are not always easy to ride.

Shetland Pony

The Shetland is small, tough, and very strong. If it is trained well, it makes a good riding pony. The Shetland is named after remote islands that lie to the northeast of Scotland.

Quarter Horse

This American horse got its name because it used to be raced over a distance of one quarter (fourth) of a mile (around 0.4km). It is very popular in Western riding.

Welsh Pony

Top tip

The beautiful Welsh Pony, or Section B, is probably the best riding pony in the world. It is perfect for shows and competitions.

Socks and stripes

Most horses and ponies have some white markings, either on their faces or on their legs—and in many cases on both. Each marking has a special name such as a sock or a stripe. These names are very useful when telling one horse or pony from another.

Star and snip

Blaze

Stripe
A long, thin white mark down a horse's face is called a stripe.

Face marks
A wide white band down a horse's face is known as a blaze, while a thin band is a stripe. A white patch on a horse's forehead is a star. On the muzzle it is called a snip.

Colors

Most horses are a shade of brown or gray and have dark skin. Some gray horses are born dark and become paler as they grow older. Each coat color has a special name.

Buckskin

Pinto

Chestnut

Palomino

Dark bay

Gray

Leg marks

If your horse has a white mark that stretches from its foot to above its knee, we say that it has a stocking. A shorter white mark is called a sock.

Bright bay

Top tip

Sock
A white mark from the foot to just below the hock or knee is called a sock.

Spotted coat
Some horses and ponies are spotted. They have dark spots on a white coat or white spots on a dark coat.

13

What to wear

Riding clothes are made to keep you safe and comfortable. The two most important items are a helmet and safe boots. You can ride in jeans, but tight-fitting jodhpurs are better because they stop your legs from being rubbed or pinched by the saddle.

Top tip

Neat hair
If you have long hair, make sure that it is tied back, braided, or tucked into a hairnet for riding. Flapping hair looks messy and gets in the way when you ride.

Helmet
Make sure that your helmet is the right size. Adjust the safety harness so that your helmet does not slip in any direction.

Gloves
These help you grip the reins. Gloves also stop your hands from becoming sore.

Jodhpurs
These pants have special patches on the insides of the knees to give you extra grip when you are riding.

Stay safe
Body protectors were first made for jockeys. They help prevent injuries if you fall. You should definitely wear one when you go jumping.

Jodhpur boots
Always wear jodhpur boots. Never ride in sneakers because the laces can easily get stuck in the stirrup irons.

Tack

A horse or pony's saddle, bridle, and any other equipment that it wears is known as tack. All tack must be kept clean and in good condition. Dirty and worn tack can make your horse or pony sore.

stirrup iron

pommel

girth

cantle

stirrup leather

saddle pad

headpiece

browband

cheekpiece

noseband

bit

throatlatch

reins

Saddle
The saddle must fit the horse perfectly. It must also be the right size for the rider.

Bridle
This is the headgear. It is made up of the headpiece and throatlatch, the browband, cheekpieces, noseband, reins, and the "bit," which fits in the horse or pony's mouth.

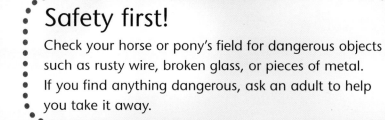

Safety first!

Check your horse or pony's field for dangerous objects such as rusty wire, broken glass, or pieces of metal. If you find anything dangerous, ask an adult to help you take it away.

Top tip

Plant alert

Many plants, such as yew, are poisonous to horses. Ask an adult to help you dig these up and get rid of them.

In the field

Horses and ponies love to wander far and wide eating grass. Today a field is the closest thing to a natural home that we can give them. They must have a trough of clean water and a shelter to protect them from wet weather or the hot sun. Cows make good companions for horses in a field.

No way out

The field must be surrounded by a strong fence to keep your horse or pony from getting out. Wooden fencing is perfect for a horse field.

Electric fence

A field may be divided into sections by electric fencing. While your horse is grazing in one part of the field, the grass in the other section has a chance to grow back.

Frisky pony

Stay away from a frisky horse or pony when it is enjoying a canter around its field.

Warm blanket

In the winter your horse may need to wear a waterproof blanket in the field in order to keep it warm, dry, and comfortable.

Clean grass

Your horse's manure may contain the eggs of worms that could make it sick. Remove the manure from the field regularly.

Lower latch

Attach a lower latch to the bottom of the door so that your horse or pony cannot get out from its stable.

Horses and ponies in stables

Being cooped up in a stable is very unnatural for an animal, but it is sometimes necessary. Horses and ponies that are fit and compete are stabled because they need to have a controlled diet. An injured or sick animal may need to be kept stabled until it is better. But stabled animals should be allowed, whenever possible, to spend part of each day in a pasture or field.

Mucking out

Keeping your horse's stable clean is a very important job. Wet bedding should be removed each morning and any manure picked up regularly during the day.

Stable blanket

In cold weather horses and ponies need a warm blanket at night. This will stay in place even if the horse or pony lies down and rolls on its side.

Freshwater

Your horse's water bucket should be emptied regularly, cleaned, and refilled with freshwater.

Bedding

The stable floor needs a good covering of bedding in order to prevent your horse or pony from hurting itself when it lies down. Straw, shredded paper, wood shavings, and rubber matting are all suitable.

Food and water

Grass is a horse's natural food. But if you ride your horse regularly, grass will not give it enough energy. Also, in the winter there are not enough nutrients in the grass, even for a horse that is not being ridden. This is why horses need hay and other foods to keep them healthy.

Haynet
A haynet stops your horse or pony from walking on the hay and wasting it.

Hanging high
Tie the haynet to a ring on the wall, high enough to stop your horse from getting its feet stuck in it.

Water
Make sure that your horse always has a supply of clean water that it can reach easily.

Top tip

Quick release
Tie the haynet to the wall with a quick-release knot. This makes it easy to undo when the haynet is empty.

Short feed
Hay and grass are called roughage and form the main part of a horse's diet. Other feeds are known as concentrated feeds. They are mixed together and fed in a bucket or manger.

Little and often

Horses need to eat a lot of food but only in small amounts. Otherwise they may become sick. Always feed your horse or pony at the same times each day, and never go riding right after feeding.

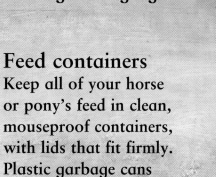

Tasty treat

Most horses love carrots. Always cut carrots lengthwise, not in rings or chunks, which could make your horse choke.

Feed containers

Keep all of your horse or pony's feed in clean, mouseproof containers, with lids that fit firmly. Plastic garbage cans are perfect.

Some types of horse and pony feeds

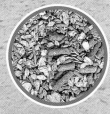

Sweet feed   Pellets   Bran   Chopped hay   Oats   Barley

Top tip

Deworming

Make sure that your horse or pony is treated regularly for worms. You can give it powder with its food or squirt a special paste into its mouth. Ask an adult to help you.

Happy and healthy

It is not difficult to tell if your horse or pony is healthy. A healthy horse has a shiny coat. It enjoys galloping around the field with its friends and is interested in what is going on around it. A horse whose coat is dull and that stands on its own, with its head down and not wanting to eat, is probably not feeling well.

Trotting

If your horse is limping, this is known as being lame. The vet will watch your horse as you walk and trot it. This helps the vet tell which leg is causing the problem.

What to look for

Press your horse's ribs with your finger. If it is the correct weight, you will be able to feel the bones but not see them. Then check your horse's ears, eyes, coat, and feet.

Alert ears
Pricked ears show that a horse is interested in what is going on around it.

Bright eyes
A healthy horse has bright eyes. Dull eyes usually mean that it is not feeling well.

Shiny coat
Your horse should have a smooth, glossy coat. If the hairs are standing up, the horse may be cold or sick.

Safety first!
If your horse starts lying down and getting up a lot and begins to sweat, it may have an illness called colic. This can be caused by eating too much. Your horse must be seen by a vet right away.

Neat feet
A horse's hooves should be trimmed regularly to stop them from cracking or growing too long.

Don't run

Horses are easily
startled by sudden
movements or
noises, so never
run up to them
or approach them
from behind.

Leading

There are times when you will need to use
a halter to lead your horse or pony—when
you get it from its field, for example. When
you go to catch your horse, make sure that
it can see and hear you coming. Walk up
to it calmly, speaking in a quiet voice.

Safety first!

Stay at a safe distance
when you are walking
with a horse that is being
led. If it is feeling frisky,
it may kick out.

On the left

When you lead a horse, walk on its left-hand side. Walk next to your horse's shoulder, not in front of it.

Safe shoes

Wear sturdy shoes or boots, not sneakers, when you are near your horse, in case it steps on your feet by accident.

Lead rope

Hold the lead rope with both hands. Don't let the end trail on the ground, or you might trip. Never wrap the rope around your hands.

Putting on the halter

1 Stand on your horse's left side. Put the rope around its neck, slide on the noseband, and grab the buckle.

2 Fasten the halter on the left side. Make sure that you pull the loose end completely through the buckle.

3 Check that the halter fits correctly—the noseband should be well above the horse's nose, not low over its nostrils.

Clean and shiny

Grooming means using different tools to brush your horse or pony's coat, pick out its hooves, and clean its eyes, nose, and around the top of its tail. Grooming helps keep a horse healthy. It also makes it look professional and keeps its tack and your clothes clean.

Plastic or rubber curry comb
This is useful for removing dried mud and loose hairs.

Grooming kit
A special grooming kit is useful for keeping all of your grooming tools together. When you are grooming, place it far away from your horse.

Top tip

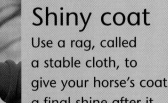

Shiny coat
Use a rag, called a stable cloth, to give your horse's coat a final shine after it has been groomed.

Dandy brush
This stiff brush is good for removing dried mud, but you should use it gently.

Body brush
This soft brush is used to groom all of the horse, including its head, mane, and tail.

Metal curry comb
Use the metal curry comb to clean the body brush. Never use it on your horse.

Sponge
Use a damp sponge to wipe around a horse's eyes and a different sponge to clean its nose.

Hoof pick
Before you go out riding, always use a hoof pick to clean your horse's feet.

Hoof oil
For special occasions brush this oil onto your horse's feet to make them shine.

Safety first!
Never kneel or sit down on the floor when you groom your horse. Bend or squat down so that you can get out of the way quickly if it makes a sudden movement.

27

Tacking up

Knowing how to put on your horse or pony's saddle and bridle—or "tacking up"—is an important part of learning how to ride. Always be gentle, never bang the saddle onto your horse's back, and be careful not to hurt its eyes or ears.

Putting on the bridle

1 Put the reins over the horse's neck. Move your right arm under its jaw and hold the bridle. With your left hand, press the bit into its mouth.

2 Carefully pass the headpiece over the horse's ears. Pull its forelock over the browband.

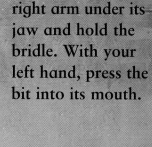

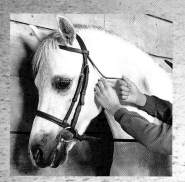

3 Fasten the throatlatch but not too tightly. You should be able to fit the full width of your hand between the throatlatch and the side of the horse's jawbone.

4 When the noseband is fastened, you should be able to slide two fingers between it and the horse's nose.

Putting on the saddle

1 Slide the saddle onto your horse's back from its left side. Make sure that the stirrup irons are at the top of the leathers and that the girth is folded over the saddle.

2 Move around the horse and lower the girth, making sure that it is not twisted. Go back to the left side and fasten the girth—but not too tightly at first.

Top tip

Saddle soap
To keep the tack clean and soft, sponge off all of the dirt and grease and then rub special saddle soap into the leather.

3 Use your hand to smooth out any wrinkles on the horse's skin underneath the girth and check that the girth is tight enough.

First lesson

Riding lessons take place in an area called the arena. In your first riding lesson you will learn how to get on and off your horse and how to hold the reins. Mounting and dismounting may seem difficult at first, but they will become much easier with practice.

Hands ahead

Hold the left rein in your left hand and your right rein in your right hand, pointing straight ahead.

Mounting

1 Stand beside your horse, holding the reins and the front of the saddle in your left hand. Take the stirrup in your right hand and put your left foot in it.

2 Grip the far side of the saddle with your right hand. Jump up, straighten both legs, and point your left toe down so that it does not dig into the horse's side.

3 Swing your right leg over the horse's back and let go of the saddle. Sit down gently in the saddle and put your right foot in the stirrup iron.

Positions, please

Sit up tall in the deepest part of the saddle. To help you maintain a good position, imagine a line running from the top of your head through your elbows and hips to your heels. Keep your head up and look to the front.

Dismounting

1 Hold the reins in your left hand. Take both feet out of the stirrups and lean forward slightly.

2 Swing your right leg up and over the saddle. Be careful not to kick your horse's back.

3 Hold the front of the saddle and slide down gently to the ground. Bend your knees as you land on your toes.

In the stirrups

Rest the balls of your feet on the stirrup irons. Your heels should be lower than your toes.

Top tip

Tight girth

To tighten the girth when mounted, hold the reins in your right hand, lift your left leg, and raise the saddle flap with your left hand.

Warming up

Mounted exercises are a lot of fun, and they help make you flexible. You will find it easier to ride if you do stretching exercises to warm up your muscles. Exercises also help improve your balance, which will give you confidence. The best time to do them is before a lesson.

Zip up

Always zip up your coat before you start exercising. Loose clothes can get caught in the saddle.

Toe touch

You can do lots of fun stretching exercises on a horse or pony. Try raising your right arm above your head and then stretch down to touch your left toe. Sit up straight and do it again, but this time touch your right toe with your left hand.

Safety first!

When you do a mounted exercise, your trainer should hold the horse to make sure that it does not move.

Around the world

This exercise looks difficult at first, but it is fun to do and is very good for your balance.

1 Begin by letting go of the reins and taking both feet out of the stirrups.

2 Hold onto the saddle and swing your right leg over the horse's neck so that you're facing sideways.

3 Swing your left leg over its back so that you are facing its tail. Be careful not to kick it.

4 Swing your right leg over so that you face the other side. Do not forget to move your hands.

5 Finally, swing your left leg over its neck. Now you are back where you began, facing forward.

33

On the move

To tell your horse or pony to move forward, turn corners, and stop, you have to use signals called "aids." If at first your horse does not do what you want, it may be because you are not giving it the correct signals.

Walk on

Before you start moving, you should be sitting up straight. To tell your horse to go from halt to walk, press its sides with your lower legs and say "Walk on."

Halt

To stop, press the horse's sides with your legs and bring your hands back toward your body. When the horse stops, relax your hold on the reins.

Take a turn

Once you know how to ask your horse to move forward and stop, you can learn how to make turns. Remember to practice turning both left and right.

Safety first!

Never pull roughly on the reins when telling your horse to turn. You could hurt its mouth.

Right hand

To turn left, move your right hand forward.

Left hand

At the same time, move your left hand outward.

Top tip

Look first

Always look in the direction you want to turn and keep your head up.

Turning left

To turn left, press your right leg against the horse's side behind the girth. Move your right hand forward so that the horse can bend its head to the left. At the same time, move your left hand outward. If you want to turn right, do the opposite movements.

Bouncy ride

To tell your horse to go from walk to trot, squeeze it with your lower legs. The trot feels less bumpy if you rise out of the saddle in time with the horse's strides. This is called a rising trot.

Sit down

Lower yourself gently into the saddle as the horse's outside foreleg hits the ground.

outside foreleg

Trot

The trot is a faster gait than the walk. When your horse trots, its feet hit the ground two at a time in diagonal pairs. This is very different from walking, when it moves its legs one at a time. The trot is the most difficult gait for the rider to learn because it feels very bumpy at first.

Safety first!

Fit a neck strap onto your horse or pony. If you start to lose your balance, hold onto the neck strap or your horse's mane.

Rise up

Lift yourself slightly out of the saddle as the horse's inside foreleg touches the ground.

inside foreleg

Up and down

When you rise to the trot in an arena, your weight should be in the saddle when the horse's outside foreleg (the leg closest to the fence) hits the ground. Lift your weight out of the saddle as its inside foreleg (the leg closest to the center of the arena) touches the ground.

Top tip

One-two

When you are first learning to trot, call out "Up-down" or "One-two" in time with your horse's strides.

Right leg first

To canter with the horse's right leg leading, keep your right leg on the girth and squeeze behind the girth with your left leg.

Leading leg

When it is cantering, a horse "leads" with its left front leg if it is circling to the left. If it is circling to the right, it leads with its right front leg.

Canter

The canter is a faster gait than the trot. It is a very comfortable gait for the rider, but you may find it a little bumpy at first. To enjoy cantering, you must learn to relax and stay seated in the saddle.

Top tip

Practice!

Before you try to canter, practice the leg positions at halt. Move your left leg behind the girth to ask the horse to lead with its right leg.

Moving hands

Keep some contact with your horse's mouth through the reins, but let your hands follow the movement of its head and neck.

Relax

In order to stay sitting down in the saddle, you must relax. This will help you follow your horse's movements.

leading leg

Gallop

Horses find it very exciting to gallop, which is the fastest gait of all. You should sit forward and slightly out of the saddle. Let the horse stretch its neck, but do not lose contact with its mouth.

Safety first!

Never gallop until you can first control your horse at walk, trot, and canter. If you gallop with other riders, leave plenty of space between each horse.

Trotting over poles

Before your first jump, walk or trot over poles on the ground. This helps you and your horse get used to the rhythm of jumping.

Look forward

Do not pull on the reins to stay balanced

Cross rails

Always use a fence with cross rails when you are learning to jump. Cross rails help your horse stay in a straight line and jump in the middle of the fence.

First jump

Jumping is one of the most exciting things that you can do with your horse or pony, but it takes practice. You should not try to jump until you have learned to walk, trot, and canter and can make turns and circles.

In position

You can practice the correct jumping position at the halt. Your lower leg should be directly under you, not swinging back or pushed forward. Remember to shorten your stirrup leathers by one or two holes when you are jumping.

Top tip

Jumping a fence

1 As your horse approaches the fence, lean forward into the jumping position. You should be sitting slightly out of the saddle.

2 At the fence the horse pushes up with its hindquarters. Follow its movement, but do not throw yourself forward. Do not drop the reins.

3 As you clear the fence, keep holding the reins but allow the horse to stretch its head and neck. Try not to bump down into the saddle.

4 The last stage of a jump is called the landing. You should be slightly out of the saddle as your horse moves away from the fence.

What is Western riding?

Western riding is based on the easygoing style of the North American cowboys. They were often on horseback all day long, driving cattle over long distances. Horses that are ridden Western style today are still taught many of the same traditional movements used by cowboys.

Headstall
A loop that fits around one ear is called a split-ear headstall.

At ease
A cowboy and his horse needed a really comfortable saddle. The Western saddle spreads the rider's weight over a large area of the horse's back.

The saddle
A Western saddle looks very different from an English saddle and is a lot heavier. You may need help to lift it onto your horse or pony's back.

cheekpiece

crownpiece

The bridle
The bridle has no noseband, and the long reins are not buckled together. Cowboys trained their horses to stand still when the reins were dropped on the ground.

Bit
The Western bit has long shanks. It must be used very gently, or otherwise it can hurt the horse or pony's mouth.

Horn
Cowboys tied a rope to the horn when they were catching cattle.

What to wear
For everyday riding you can wear loose-fitting, casual clothes, such as a pair of jeans and a shirt, with jodhpur boots or cowboy boots.

Top tip

Hard hat
Cowboys traditionally wore a broad-brimmed hat, but for safety you should always wear a riding helmet with a chinstrap.

cantle

back jockey

skirt

seat jockey

fender

latigo

cinch

Stirrups
Western stirrups are wooden or plastic and are sometimes covered with leather.

The Western seat
Sit in the deepest part of the saddle, with a long stirrup so that your leg is fairly straight.

One hand
If you are left-handed, the ends of the reins hang on the left side of the horse, and if you are right-handed, they hang on the right side.

Stirrups
Position your foot so that the stirrup is under the ball of your foot, just behind your toes.

Top tip

Halting
To stop, push your weight down into the stirrups and calmly say "Whoa." Do not shout at your horse.

Western riding
Western riders hold their hands fairly high—slightly in front of the horn of the saddle, at around the same height as their hips. Beginners should ride with two hands on the reins. This makes it easier to stay balanced and in the correct position. Soon you will be able to ride with only one hand, with your free hand resting on your thigh.

Walking

To move from halt to walk, make a clicking noise with your tongue and press the horse's sides lightly with your legs.

Light reins

Hold the reins very lightly, and never pull on them. On a well-trained horse the slightest signal with the reins should be enough to tell it what to do.

Mounting Western style

1 Face the horse's side. Place your left hand on its neck and put your left foot in the stirrup.

2 Grip the saddle with your right hand and jump up from your right foot.

3 Swing your right leg high up over the horse's back, being careful not to kick it.

Top tip

Dismount

Hold the horn with your right hand, swing your right leg over, and place your foot on the ground. Then take your left foot out of the stirrup.

The lope

To go from a jog or a trot into a lope, squeeze the horse with your lower legs. Use your right leg on the girth to ask the horse to lead with its left leg or use your left leg to ask it to lead with its right leg.

Slowing down

When you want to slow down from a lope to a jog or from a jog to a walk, move your shoulders back a little and raise your hand slightly.

Western gaits

The basic gaits in Western riding are the walk, the jog, and the lope. The jog is a slow, relaxed trot. The lope is a steady canter. When cowboys rode at a fast trot, they often used to stand up in the stirrups, holding onto the horn of the saddle with one hand in order to keep their balance.

The jog

To move from a walk to a jog, click with your tongue and press the horse's sides lightly with your lower legs. Relax the pressure as soon as the horse changes gait.

Trail riding

Going for a ride in the countryside is a lot of fun. Horses and ponies like to see new places too. You can explore woods and fields or canter along a trail with your friends.

Hands up

If your horse does not stop when you say "Whoa," raise your hands a little in order to put pressure on the bit.

Safety first!

Until you are older, it is best to have an adult with you when you go out riding. They can help if you find the horse or pony difficult to control.

Index

Acknowledgments

The publisher would like to thank the following for their help in the production of this book:

Models: Charley, Ellie, Elliot, Fraser, Hollie, Nirvana, and Rhianna

Ponies: Chip, Jasper, Pickwick, Piglet, Pikie, Prince, Silver, and Teddy

The Justine Armstrong-Small team (www.armstrong-small.co.uk): Justine and Hazel Armstrong-Small Grooms: Amy, Becky, Katie, Keeley, Lisa, Rosie, and Vicky

Dublin, Cuddly Ponies, and Roma (www.weatherbeeta.com)

Photography: Matthew Roberts (www.matthewrobertsphotographer.com)

David and Sarah Deptford (www.sovereignquarterhorses.com)

The Ada Cole Rescue Stables (www.adacole.co.uk)

All at Bumbles Green Farm

All photographs by Matthew Roberts with the exception of: page 10cl, 10tr, 11tr, 11cr, 13br, 16bl, 27tr, 45bl, 47tl (Bob Langrish, www.boblangrish.co.uk)